HIGH-OCTANE CAREERS

FIGHTER JET PILOT

BY THEIA LAKE

Gareth Stevens PUBLISHING

HOT TOPICS

Please visit our website, www.garethstevens.com. For a free color catalog of all our high-quality books, call toll free 1-800-542-2595 or fax 1-877-542-2596.

Cataloging-in-Publication Data

Names: Lake, Theia.
Title: Fighter jet pilot / Theia Lake.
Description: Buffalo, NY : Gareth Stevens Publishing, 2025. | Series: High-octane careers | Includes glossary.
Identifiers: ISBN 9781482469264 (pbk.) | ISBN 9781482469271 (library bound) | ISBN 9781482469288 (ebook)
Subjects: LCSH: Fighter planes–Piloting–Juvenile literature. | Fighter pilots–Vocational guidance–United States–Juvenile literature. | Jet planes, Military–Juvenile literature.
Classification: LCC UG1242.F5 L25 2025 | DDC 623.74'64–dc23

Published in 2025 by
Gareth Stevens Publishing
2544 Clinton Street
Buffalo, NY 14224

Designer: Claire Zimmermann
Editor: Theresa Emminizer

Photo credits: Cover, pp. 1 (man), 16, 19 PeopleImages.com - Yuri A/Shutterstock.com; cover, p.1 (jet background) Aqeela_Image/Shutterstock.com; cover, p. 1 (lower photo) Anjar G/Shutterstock.com; cover, p.1 (series title light flare) SpicyTruffel/Shutterstock.com; series art (background texture) Golubovy/Shutterstock.com; p. 5 Zoteva/Shutterstock.com; p. 7 dcwcreations/Shutterstock.com; p. 8 TEEREXZ/Shutterstock.com; p. 9 aappp/Shutterstock.com; p. 11 Jaroslav Moravcik/Shutterstock.com; p. 13 Aerial-motion/Shutterstock.com; p. 15 Soos Jozsef/Shutterstock.com; p. 17 LapailrKrapai/Shutterstock.com; p. 21 University of College/Shutterstock.com; p. 23 U.S. Navy Photo by Mass Communication Specialist Seaman Marco Villasana/Released; p. 25 U.S. Navy photo by Mass Communication Specialist 3rd Class DJ Revell/Released; p. 27 bekirevren/Shutterstock.com; p. 29 SeventyFour/Shutterstock.com; p. 30 (icons) top dog/Shutterstock.com.

CONTENTS

SKY HIGH!

Do you find yourself drawn to the skies? Can you picture yourself flying through the air at eye-watering speeds? If so, you might want to be a fighter jet pilot! Fighter jet pilots fly superfast jet planes in combat, or battle.

UNDER PRESSURE!

Jets are powered by special **engines** that use air and **fuel** to propel (push) the aircraft forward. Jets can reach greater speeds and heights than other planes.

FLYING FOR THE FORCES

The U.S. Air Force, Marine Corps, and Navy are three branches of the U.S. military, or armed forces, that have fighter jet pilots. These pilots do air-to-air and air-to-ground combat missions. A mission is a job with a particular objective.

UNDER PRESSURE!

U.S. Army and Coast Guard pilots don't usually fly fighter jets. Instead, they usually fly other kinds of aircraft, such as **helicopters**.

GROUNDWORK

Fighter pilots do a lot of groundwork before they take flight. First, they study the mission brief, or plan. They study the location, or area, where they'll be flying and its weather. They gather gear and check the aircraft before flight.

UNDER PRESSURE!

After a pilot comes back from their mission, they also meet with their team to debrief, or talk about what happened.

SUITING UP

Fighter pilots wear special gear to keep them safe:

- A **fire-resistant** flight suit.
- An **antigravity** suit called a G-Suit.
- A helmet with an oxygen (air) mask.
- Night vision (seeing) glasses.
- A harness (straps to hold them in place).
- A **parachute**.

UNDER PRESSURE!

Pilots wear a device, or tool, to help them float if they land in water. They also carry a knife, a flashlight, and a compass.

IN THE COCKPIT

The cockpit is the part of the plane where the pilot sits and operates the aircraft. Pilots are supposed to spend a certain number of hours in flight. In addition to fighting, pilots may gather intel, or facts, and take pictures of enemy forces.

UNDER PRESSURE!

Navy and Marine fighter pilots take off from and land on large ships called aircraft carriers. They may fly very close to the sea looking for underwater threats, or dangers.

DOGFIGHTING

Close aerial (sky) combat between aircraft is called dogfighting. During a dogfight, pilots must do skillful **maneuvers** to beat their opponent, or enemy. Today, **technology** has changed air-to-air combat. New Helmet Mounted Displays (HMDs) show pilots key information and help them take better aim.

UNDER PRESSURE!

In the past, many fighter jets were armed with machine guns. Today, they're also armed with guided air-to-air missiles.

ENLISTING

The first step to becoming a pilot is to enlist, or sign up to join, the armed forces. To join the military, you must be a U.S. citizen. You need to be at least 17 years old and have a high school **diploma**.

UNDER PRESSURE!

A recruiter is someone who finds people to enlist in the armed forces. Recruiters often come to schools to give students information about military careers.

PHYSICAL REQUIREMENTS

Air Force pilots must meet certain physical (body) requirements:

- Pilots can't be much shorter or taller than average.
- They must have perfect hearing.
- They must have normal color vision (not colorblind).
- They have near-perfect vision.

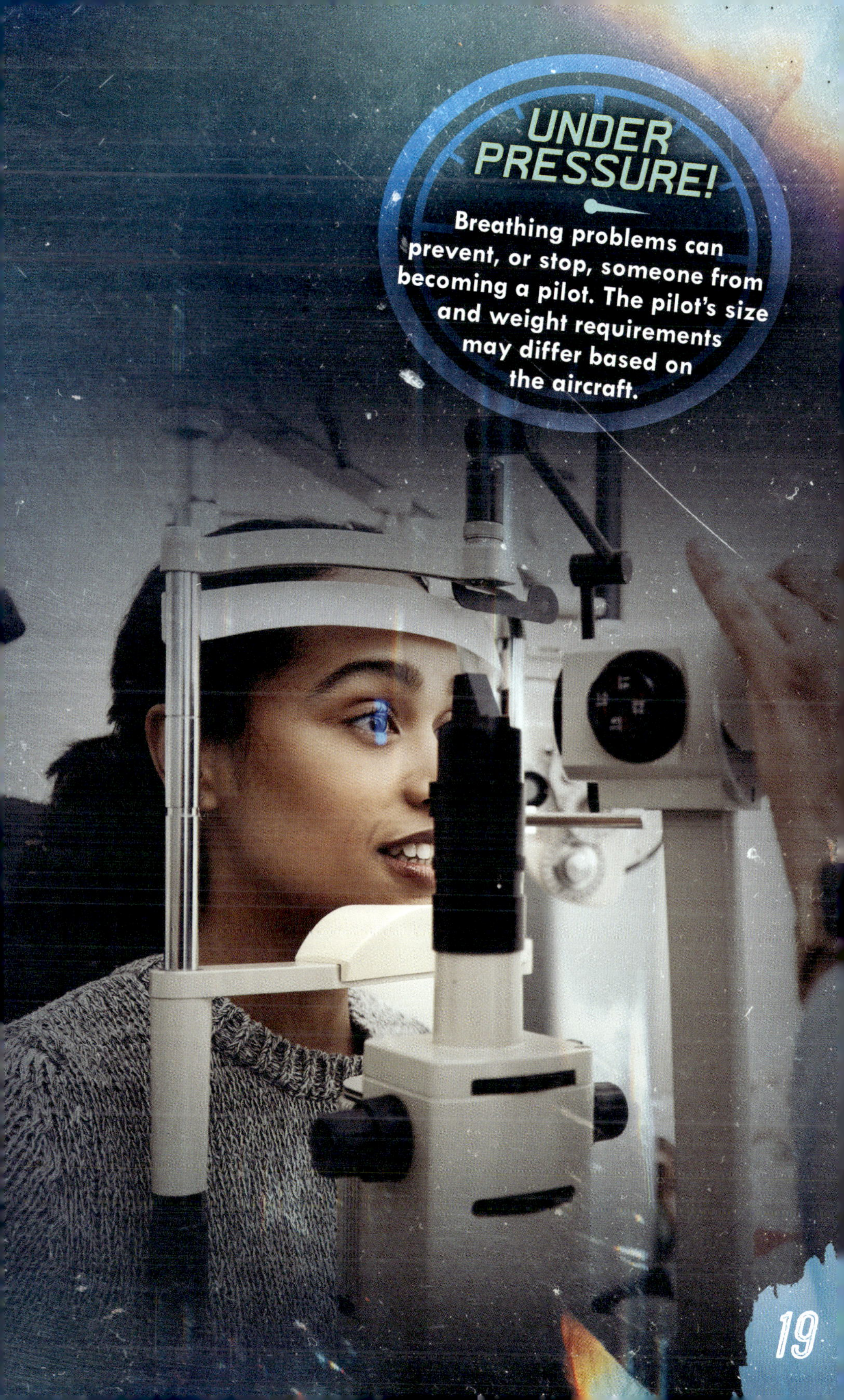

UNDER PRESSURE!

Breathing problems can prevent, or stop, someone from becoming a pilot. The pilot's size and weight requirements may differ based on the aircraft.

EDUCATION

Military recruits need to pass a background test and written test. Air Force officers must have a bachelor's (four year) degree. They must go to Officer Training School or the Air Force Academy and pass the Air Force Officer Qualifying Test.

UNDER PRESSURE!

The U.S. Air Force, Navy, and Marines offer programs to help recruits get the education they need to advance, or move forward, in their career paths.

GETTING YOUR WINGS

Pilots must pass a basic flight training program before they can enter an Undergraduate Pilot Training (UPT) program. In UPT, pilots learn how to navigate, fly in formation, and more. Near the end of the UPT, pilots are assigned an aircraft and seat.

UNDER PRESSURE!

Fighter pilots have to be able to go through pressure changes in flight without throwing up or passing out. This pressure is measured as G-force, or the force of gravity.

ACTIVE DUTY

The Navy, Marines, and Air Force have different requirements about active duty, or full-time military service. Most pilots are committed to active duty for 8 to 10 years. Fighter pilots may receive retention pay, which is a bonus for staying in active service.

UNDER PRESSURE!

In 2023, the average salary for a military fighter pilot was about $89,700 per year. More experienced pilots may earn more than this.

SPECIAL SKILLS

Fighter pilots must be quick thinkers and good problem solvers. Above all, they must keep calm under pressure. In the cockpit, a fighter pilot may fly at a speed of more than 1,000 miles (1,609 km) per hour, launch a missile, and maneuver their aircraft all at the same time.

UNDER PRESSURE!

Fighter pilots operate, or use, some of the most advanced technology in the world. This takes strong skills and knowledge in science, math, and reasoning.

THE SKY IS THE LIMIT

Do you think you've got what it takes to become a fighter jet pilot? You don't have to wait until flight school to get started. Build your skills in math and science. Keep fit and strong. Learn about different kinds of aircraft and how they work.

UNDER PRESSURE!

Visit your library and check out books about flight history and aircraft! Learn as much as you can about aviation, or the art of flying aircraft.

AIRCRAFT TOP SPEEDS

Aircraft speed is measured in Mach, or the speed of sound. Mach 1 is 761 miles (1,224.7 km) per hour.

AIR FORCE JETS

F-15 EAGLE
Mach 3

F-16 FIGHTING FALCON
Mach 2

F-22 RAPTOR
Mach 2.5

F-35A LIGHTNING II
Mach 1.6

NAVY AND MARINE CORPS JETS

F-18 HORNET
Mach 1.8

F-35 LIGHTNING
Mach 1.6

FOR MORE INFORMATION

BOOKS

Bolte, Mari. *Fighter Jets in Action.* Minneapolis, MN: Lerner Publications, 2024.

Schuh, Mari H. *Military Aircraft.* North Mankato, MN: Pebble, a Capstone imprint, 2023.

WEBSITES

Air Force
www.airforce.com/careers/aviation-and-flight/pilot
Learn about what it takes to become a U.S. Air Force pilot!

Navy
www.navy.com/careers-benefits/careers/aviation/fighter-pilot
Find out about a career as a U.S. Navy fighter pilot.

GLOSSARY

antigravity: Lessening or protecting against the effect of gravity.

compass: A tool for finding directions by using a magnetic needle.

diploma: An official paper showing that a student has finished a course of study.

engine: A machine that makes power.

fire-resistant: Made to stop or protect against fire.

fuel: Something used to make energy, heat, or power.

helicopter: An aircraft that uses spinning blades to fly.

maneuver: A way of moving.

missile: A rocket used to strike something at a distance.

parachute: A specially shaped piece of cloth that collects air to slow something down.

technology: Using science, engineering, and other industries to invent useful tools or to solve problems. Also a machine, piece of equipment, or method created by technology.

INDEX